Practice to Learn

ALPHABET

Editor in Chief/Project Director: Karen J. Goldfluss, M.S. Ed.

Editor: Eric Migliaccio

Co-Authors: Katy Pike, Eric Migliaccio

Imaging: James Edward Grace

Cover and Interior Design: Sarah Kim

Art Coordinator: Renee Mc Elwee

Creative Director: Sarah M. Fournier

Publisher: Mary D. Smith, M.S. Ed.

Teacher Created Resources
12621 Western Avenue
Garden Grove, CA 92841
Printed in U.S.A.

www.teachercreated.com
ISBN: 978-1-4206-8202-1
©2019 Teacher Created Resources
Made in U.S.A.

Dear Parent,

This book is part of the *Practice to Learn* series for young learners. Each vibrant book in the series includes a wide range of interesting activities that will help your child develop essential foundational skills. Written by experienced teachers and educators, the series supports what your child learns at school.

The pages are clear and uncluttered, with activities that build real skills. Activities are fun and motivate children to continue working and learning. Instructions are clear and easy to follow.

We hope that you and your child enjoy using this and other books in the series.

Contents

Around the House

Use what you already have and what you already do in and around the house to help your child practice and learn the alphabet at home.

▶ **Name that Food** — With your child, find a food for each letter of the alphabet. Together, create a Tasty Alphabet book.

▶ **An Animal Alphabet** — Find an animal for each letter of the alphabet and create a book for them, as well.

▶ **Write on the Fridge** — The inside of a refrigerator has a job to do, and now you can put the outside of your refrigerator to work, too. Allow your child to play with magnetic letters on the fridge by placing them in alphabetical order or by using them to form short words. You can make this into a game by removing one letter from the alphabet and asking your child to figure out which letter is missing. Consider making this game a part of a daily routine at breakfast or dinner.

▶ **Sculpting and Shaping** — Kids love to work with arts and crafts. Ask your child to use play dough to make each letter shape. Letters can then be used to form small words. Or, try asking your child to decorate each letter so that it looks like something that starts with that letter. (For example, they could add a leaf to an a to make it look like an apple.) Other items around the house can also be used to form letters. Try bending pipe cleaners or other craft materials into the shapes of letters.

▶ **Name that Thing** — In addition to recognizing the shapes of letters, children also need to know the sounds of letters. Work on this skill by asking your child to name objects in and around your home. Ask them to name the sound the word begins with. Help them with this skill until they have mastered it. Then begin to ask about ending sounds.

Shall We Play a Game?

Practicing the alphabet can be fun! Try these games and challenges:

▶ **Rainbow Letters** — Draw a large letter in the middle of a blank piece of paper. Ask your child to use different crayons to trace the letter until a rainbow effect is created.

▶ **Concentration** — Write uppercase letters on one set of flashcards and lowercase letters on another. Shuffle the cards and lay them facedown. The child turns over one card at a time and tries to find a matching pair.

▶ **Scavenger Hunt** — Attach a piece of paper to a clipboard and create a checklist by writing up to 10 letters on it. Write those same letters on sticky notes, one per note. While your child is not looking, hide the notes around your house. Have your child carry around the clipboard while searching for the hidden letters. As each is found, your child should say the letter aloud and cross it off the checklist.

▶ **Three in a Row** — Create a 3 x 3 grid and fill it with nine letters of the alphabet. Write matching letters on flashcards. Select a flashcard and read the letter on it aloud. Your child should cross off the corresponding letter on the grid. To complete the game, three letters should be found going across, down, or diagonally. You can expand this game by creating a grid with five columns and playing a traditional game of Bingo.

▶ **Under Construction** — See if your child can use the letters of the alphabet to build sight words. On flashcards, write the letters of the alphabet, one letter per card. (The letters *q*, *x*, or *z* may not be needed.) Put the cards in a pile and see how many cards your child needs to draw before being able to spell a sight word.

▶ **Alphabet Freeze Boogie** — On index cards, write all the uppercase and lowercase letters of the alphabet (one letter per card). Tape the letters to the floor all over the room. Get ready to play your child's favorite music. Explain that when the music is playing, she gets to dance, but when the music stops you will give her instructions. Then, start the music and let the fun begin! When you stop the music the first time, ask your child to find the first letter of her name. When the music stops the next time, ask her to find the second letter, and so on.

The Alphabet Is Out of this World!

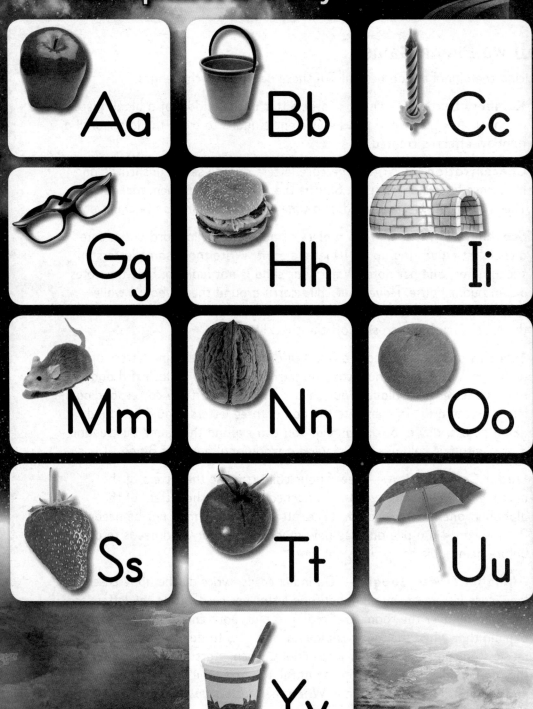

Aa Bb Cc

Gg Hh Ii

Mm Nn Oo

Ss Tt Uu

Yy

Dd

Ee

Ff

Jj

Kk

Ll

Pp

Qq

Rr

Vv

Ww

Xx

Zz

Aa

Trace and write.

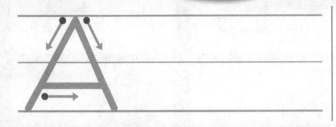
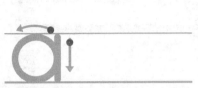

Circle every A.

A   B   **A**   **E**

T   **A**   N   A

How many? _____

Circle every a.

a   g   **n**   a

c   a   o   a

How many? _____

Add a and then say the word.

_____pple

_____nt

8

Circle the pictures that begin with a.

Can you find all 7?

Circle every a you see.

a p e   c a t   c r a b

CHALLENGE

Can you turn an a into art? Draw on the a to make it look like an animal.

a

9

Bb

Trace and write.

B

b

Circle every B.

B A **P** **B**

B **D** O R

How many? _____

Circle every b.

b b **d** p

a b **e** b

How many? _____

Add b and then say the word.

_____ all

_____ ook

Bb

Circle the pictures that begin with b.

Can you find all 7?

Circle every b you see.

b e l l   b i k e   c r a b

CHALLENGE
How many beads can you draw on the string?

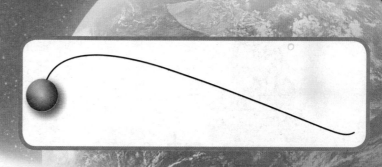

Cc

Trace and write.

C   c

Circle every C.

C   C   **C**   **A**

B   **0**   C   D

How many? _____

Circle every c.

c   q   **c**   c

b   c   a   c

How many? _____

Add c and then say the word.

_____ at

_____ arrot

Cc

Circle the pictures that begin with c.

Can you find all 6?

Circle every c you see.

cat

cow

clock

CHALLENGE Name things that begin with c.

Something you eat _____

Something you wear _____

Dd

Trace and write.

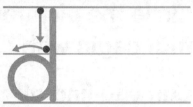

Circle every D.

D **B** **D** D

C D 0 J

How many? _____

Circle every d.

d b **d** d

d **a** e b

How many? _____

Add d and then say the word.

_____ uck

_____ oor

Dd

Circle the pictures that begin with d.

Can you find all 7?

Circle every d you see.

d o g   d o l p h i n   c a n d l e

CHALLENGE Draw the dots on the dice.

1	2	3	4	5	6
dot	dots	dots	dots	dots	dots

Ee

Trace and write.

Circle every E.	Circle every e.
E E E R	e c e e
C D F E	a e o e
How many? _____	How many? _____

Add e and then say the word.

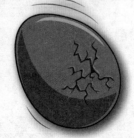
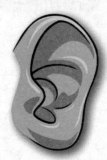

_____gg

_____ar

Ee

Circle the pictures that begin with e.

Can you find all 7?

Circle every e you see.

e g g   k e y   e l e p h a n t

CHALLENGE

Draw as many eggs as you can in the big box. How many did you draw?

eggs

Ff

Trace and write.

Circle every F.

F   F   **F**   Z

B   **E**   A   F

How many? _____

Circle every f.

f   i   f   **f**

f   j   t   f

How many? _____

Add f and then say the word.

____rog

____ish

Ff

Circle the pictures that begin with f.

Can you find all 7?

Circle every f you see.

feather   fox   fork

CHALLENGE Name things that begin with f.

a number _____

an animal _____

Gg

Trace and write.

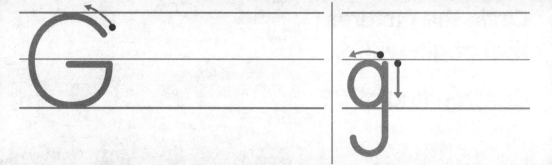

Circle every G.

O G **G** C

G G **Q** G

How many? _____

Circle every g.

g g y g

j b a g

How many? _____

Add g and then say the word.

_____ irl

_____ uitar

G g

Circle the pictures that begin with g.

Can you find all 6?

Circle every g you see.

g o a t   e g g   g u i t a r

CHALLENGE **Name things that begin with g.**

a color _____

an animal _____

a fruit _____

Hh

Trace and write.

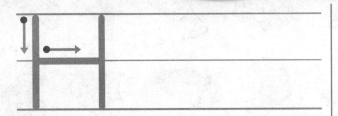

Circle every H.

H H N T
I H H H

How many? _____

Circle every h.

h m t h
h n h y

How many? _____

Add h and then say the word.

_____ en

_____ at

Hh

Circle the pictures that begin with h.

Can you find all 7?

Circle every h you see.

hippo   house   rhino

CHALLENGE Draw different hair on each head.

Trace and write.

Circle every I.

I   **I**   **L**   **F**

T   J   I   V

How many? _____

Circle every i.

i   i   **t**   j

i   t   *i*   **i**

How many? _____

Add i and then say the word.

_____ce

_____nsects

24

Ii

Circle the pictures that begin with i.

Can you find all 7?

Circle every i you see.

i c e   i t c h   l i o n

CHALLENGE Write one thing about yourself. Start with I.

25

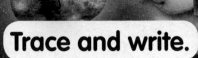

Jj

Trace and write.

J   j

Circle every J.

J   J   **G**   L

J   **Y**   J   J

How many? _____

Circle every j.

j   **j**   g   j

y   j   j   i

How many? _____

Add j and then say the word.

_____et

_____eans

Circle the pictures that begin with j.

Can you find all 6?

Circle every j you see.

j a r   j u g   j u i c e

CHALLENGE Name things that begin with j.

a food you could eat

_____

a thing you could do

_____

Kk

Trace and write.

K

k

Circle every K.

K   K   R   K

H   **L**   L   K   *E*

How many? _____

Circle every k.

k   k   *k*   **w**

I   r   d   k

How many? _____

Add k and then say the word.

____oala

____ey

Kk

Circle the pictures that begin with k.

Can you find all 6?

Circle every k you see.

k i t t e n   k o a l a   b a s k e t

CHALLENGE See how many kites you can draw and color.

Ll

Trace and write.

Circle every L.

L N F L
L L I J

How many? _____

Circle every I.

I n t f
l i t l

How many? _____

Add l and then say the word.

_____ emon

_____ izard

LI

Circle the pictures that begin with l.

Can you find all 7?

Circle every l you see.

leaf   lollipop   ball

CHALLENGE

Draw a ladybug with three spots.

Draw a lollipop with three colors.

Mm

Trace and write.

M   m

Circle every M.

M E R M
D M M Z

How many? _____

Circle every m.

m h n y
m n m m

How many? _____

Add m and then say the word.

_____ oon

_____ ouse

Mm

Circle the pictures that begin with m.

Can you find all 6?

Circle every m you see.

m a s k   m a r b l e s   t o m a t o

CHALLENGE

How many foods can you think of that start with m? Write them.

33

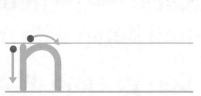

Nn

Trace and write.

Circle every N.

N N **Z** M

H **M** N N

How many? _____

Circle every n.

m n **h** n

h **n** m r

How many? _____

Add n and then say the word.

_____ut

_____est

34

Nn

Circle the pictures that begin with n.

Can you find all 6?

Circle every n you see.

numbers

ant

penguin

CHALLENGE Write nine names you know.

Trace and write.

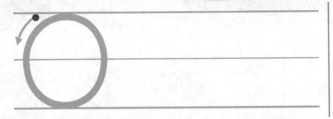

Circle every O.

O   c   **O**   O

O   D   Q   U

How many? _____

Circle every o.

o   *o*   o   **e**

a   *o*   p   o

How many? _____

Add o and then say the word.

_____range

_____ctopus

Oo

Circle the pictures that begin with o.

Can you find all 6?

Circle every o you see.

b a l l o o n   o i l   t o m a t o

CHALLENGE Name 8 orange things.

Pp

Trace and write.

Circle every P.

P	P	**P**	B
P	**B**	D	P

How many? _____

Circle every p.

p	p	b	g
j	b	**p**	p

How many? _____

Add p and then say the word.

_____ eas

_____ ear

P p

Circle the pictures that begin with p.

Can you find all 7?

Circle every p you see.

a p p l e   p i z z a   l o l l i p o p

CHALLENGE How many pairs do you see?

I see

Qq

Trace and write.

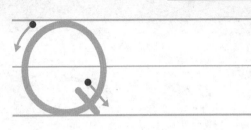

Circle every Q.

Q   C   **E**   O

Q   O   Q   P

How many? _____

Circle every q.

q   q   p   t

a   r   q   b

How many? _____

Add q and then say the word.

_____ueen

_____uack

Qq

Circle the pictures that begin with q.

Can you find all 6?

Circle every q you see.

queen   question   square

CHALLENGE Solve this rhyming riddle.
When spelling a word with a letter q,
The letter you usually see next is a

Rr

Trace and write.

R   r

Circle every R.

R   P   **B**   R
T   R   R   A

How many? _____

Circle every r.

r   r   r   g
t   i   n   r

How many? _____

Add r and then say the word.

____ing

____obot

Rr

Circle the pictures that begin with r.

Can you find all 6?

Circle every r you see.

c a r r o t   r a t   h a m b u r g e r

CHALLENGE How many red things can you name? Write them.

Ss

Trace and write.

Ŝ

ŝ

Circle every S.

S   **S**   **C**   S

J   S   S   U

How many? _____

Circle every s.

s   s   **b**   c

a   r   **s**   s

How many? _____

Add s and then say the word.

_____ un

_____ poon

Ss

Circle the pictures that begin with s.

Can you find all 9?

Circle every s you see.

scooter   seal   glasses

Tt

Trace and write.

Circle every T.

T v Z T

N T I T

How many? _____

Circle every t.

t t e i

i t t t

How many? _____

Add t and then say the word.

_____ent

_____ree

T t

Circle the pictures that begin with t.

Can you find all 6?

Circle every t you see.

tomato   toothbrush   butterfly

CHALLENGE Name 8 things that begin with t.

Uu

Trace and write.

U   u

Circle every U.

U   A   V   U
S   U   U   O

How many? _____

Circle every u.

u   c   n   u
a   u   m   v

How many? _____

Add u and then say the word.

____mbrella

____nicorn

Uu

Circle the pictures that begin with u.

Can you find all 6?

Circle every u you see.

unicycle

guitar

lettuce

CHALLENGE
Think of a tool that is very useful. Draw it.

Vv

Trace and write.

Circle every V.

V V U w

L W V V

How many? _____

Circle every v.

v v z v

n v w w

How many? _____

Add v and then say the word.

____iolin

____olcano

Vv

Circle the pictures that begin with v.

Can you find all 6?

Circle every v you see.

v a c u u m   v i o l i n   a v o c a d o

Ww

Trace and write.

W

w

Circle every W.

W   **w**   **H**   V

A   W   V   W

How many? _____

Circle every w.

w   w   V   w

u   v   w   r

How many? _____

Add w and then say the word.

_____ eb

_____ orm

Ww

Circle the pictures that begin with w.

Can you find all 7?

Circle every w you see.

water

flower

sandwich

CHALLENGE Name things that begin with w.

a season

a drink

an animal

Xx

Trace and write.

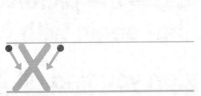

Circle every X.

X M O X

L X X X

How many? _____

Circle every x.

x x i X

t x m x

How many? _____

Add x and then say the word.

bo ____

si ____

Xx

Circle the pictures that **end** with **x**.

Can you find all 5?

Circle every **x** you see.

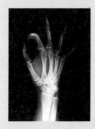

x – r a y   f o x   m i x e r

CHALLENGE
X marks the spot! Work your way through the maze to make it to the **X**.

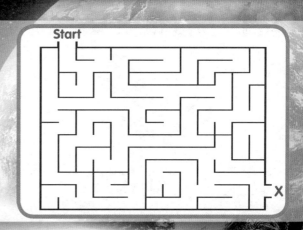

Start

x

Yy

Trace and write.

Y   y

Circle every Y.

Y   Y   **Y**   T

I   **V**   w   Y

How many? _____

Circle every y.

Y   **g**   o   y

o   **y**   u   y

How many? _____

Add y and then say the word.

 _____ellow

 _____oyo

Yy

Circle the pictures that begin with y.

Can you find all 5?

Circle every y you see.

y a k   y o g u r t   b i c y c l e

CHALLENGE Name 9 yellow things.

Zz

Trace and write.

Z   Z

Circle every Z.

Z Z S Z

N M Z I

How many? _____

Circle every z.

z z t s

z m z z

How many? _____

Add z and then say the word.

____ ebra

____ oo

Zz

Circle the pictures that begin with z.

Can you find all 6?

Circle every z you see.

zigzag

lizard

pizza

CHALLENGE Name 10 zoo animals.

Connect A–N

Connect the dots in order. Start at A. Some letters are uppercase. Some are lowercase.

Connect the dots in order. Start at **N**. Some letters are uppercase. Some are lowercase.

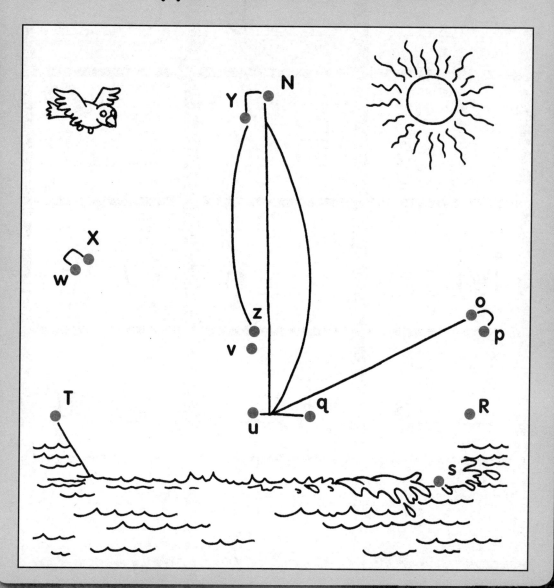

Fill Them In

A__   __b   C__

__g   H__   __i

M__   __n   O__

__s   T__   __u

__y

Fill Them In

___ d

E ___

___ f

J ___

___ k

L ___

___ p

Q ___

___ r

V ___

___ w

X ___

Z ___

63

Wow!!!

You're an alphabet superstar!